Cambridge English:
Key 6

*Official examination papers
from University of Cambridge
ESOL Examinations*

CAMBRIDGE
UNIVERSITY PRESS

CAMBRIDGE
UNIVERSITY PRESS

University Printing House, Cambridge CB2 8BS, United Kingdom

Cambridge University Press is part of the University of Cambridge.

It furthers the University's mission by disseminating knowledge in the pursuit of education, learning and research at the highest international levels of excellence.

www.cambridge.org
Information on this title: www.cambridge.org/9781107606050

© Cambridge University Press 2012

It is normally necessary for written permission for copying to be obtained
in advance from a publisher. The candidate answer sheets
at the back of this book are designed to be copied and distributed in class.
The normal requirements are waived here and it is not necessary to write to
Cambridge University Press for permission for an individual teacher to make copies
for use within his or her own classroom. Only those pages that carry the wording
'© UCLES 2012 Photocopiable ' may be copied.

First published 2012
7th printing 2015

Printed in Italy by Rotolito Lombarda S.p.A.

A catalogue record for this publication is available from the British Library

ISBN 978-1-107-60605-0 Student's Book without answers
ISBN 978-1-107-67971-9 Student's Book with answers
ISBN 978-1-107-67984-9 Audio CD
ISBN 978-1-107-69165-0 Self-study Pack

Cambridge University Press has no responsibility for the persistence or accuracy
of URLs for external or third-party internet websites referred to in this publication,
and does not guarantee that any content on such websites is, or will remain,
accurate or appropriate. Information regarding prices, travel timetables, and other
factual information given in this work is correct at the time of first printing but
Cambridge University Press does not guarantee the accuracy of such information
thereafter.

Contents

Acknowledgements

The authors and publishers acknowledge the following sources of photographs

p. 17 Tao Images/Robert Harding; p. 20 Richard Wong/Alamy; p. 22 Edward Bock/Corbis; p. 37 Greg Balfour Evans/Alamy; p. 40 Image Source/Corbis; p. 42 Lockwood_Dattatri/ naturepl.com; p. 57 PCN Photography/Alamy; p. 60 Antographer/Alamy; p. 62 Gavin Hellier/ Alamy; p. 77 amana images inc./Alamy; p. 80 AlamyCelebrity/Alamy; p. 82 Design Pics/ Ben Welsh/Getty Images

Picture research by Joanne Robinson

Book design by Peter Ducker MSTD

Cover design by David Lawton

The CD which accompanies this book was recorded at dsound, London.

A guide to Cambridge English: Key

Cambridge English: Key, also known as the *Key English Test (KET)*, is part of a comprehensive range of exams developed by University of Cambridge ESOL Examinations (Cambridge ESOL). Cambridge English exams have similar characteristics but are designed for different purposes and different levels of English language ability. *Cambridge English: Key* is at Level A2 (Waystage) of the Council of Europe's Common European Framework of Reference for Languages (CEFR). It has also been accredited in the UK as an Entry Level 2 ESOL certificate in the UK's National Qualifications Framework.

Examination	Council of Europe Framework Level	UK National Qualifications Framework Level
Cambridge English: Proficiency *Certificate of Proficiency in English (CPE)*	C2	3
Cambridge English: Advanced *Certificate in Advanced English (CAE)*	C1	2
Cambridge English: First *First Certificate in English (FCE)*	B2	1
Cambridge English: Preliminary *Preliminary English Test (PET)*	B1	Entry 3
Cambridge English: Key *Key English Test (KET)*	A2	Entry 2

Cambridge English: Key is accepted by employers, further education and government departments for business, study and immigration purposes. It is also useful preparation for higher level exams, such as *Cambridge English: Preliminary* and *Cambridge English: First*.

Cambridge English: Key is a great first step in English. Preparing for the exam will build your confidence in dealing with everyday written and spoken English at a basic level, for example expressing and understanding simple opinions; filling in forms; and writing short, simple letters.

Cambridge English: Key is also available in a version with exam content and topics specifically targeted at the interests and experience of school-aged learners. *Cambridge English: Key for Schools*, also known as the *Key English Test (KET) for Schools*, follows exactly the same format and level and leads to the same certificate as *Cambridge English: Key*.

Topics

These are the topics used in the *Cambridge English: Key* exam:

Clothes	People	Shopping
Daily life	Personal feelings, opinions	Social interaction
Entertainment and media	and experiences	The natural world
Food and drink	Personal identification	Transport
Health, medicine and exercise	Places and buildings	Travel and holidays
Hobbies and leisure	School and study	Weather
House and home	Services	Work and jobs
Language		

Overview of the exam

Paper	Name	Timing	Content	Test focus
Paper 1	Reading/ Writing	1 hour 10 minutes	Nine parts: Five parts (Parts 1–5) test a range of reading skills with a variety of texts, ranging from very short notices to longer continuous texts. Parts 6–9 concentrate on testing basic writing skills.	Assessment of candidates' ability to understand the meaning of written English at word, phrase, sentence, paragraph and whole text level. Assessment of candidates' ability to produce simple written English, ranging from one-word answers to a short piece of continuous text.
Paper 2	Listening	30 minutes (including 8 minutes transfer time)	Five parts, ranging from short exchanges to longer dialogues and monologues.	Assessment of candidates' ability to understand dialogues and monologues in both informal and neutral settings on a range of everyday topics.
Paper 3	Speaking	8–10 minutes per pair of candidates	Two parts: In Part 1, candidates interact with an examiner. In Part 2, they interact with another candidate.	Assessment of candidates' ability to answer and ask questions about themselves and about factual, non-personal information.

Paper 1   Reading and Writing

Paper format

The Reading section contains five parts. The Writing section contains four parts.

Number of questions

There is a total of 56 questions: 35 in Reading and 21 in Writing.

Sources

Authentic and adapted-authentic real-world notices, newspaper and magazine articles, simplified encyclopaedia entries.

Answering

Candidates indicate answers either by shading lozenges (Reading) or by writing answers (Writing) on an answer sheet.

Timing

1 hour 10 minutes.

Marks

Each item carries one mark, except for question 56 (Part 9), which is marked out of 5. This gives a total of 60 marks, which is weighted to a final mark out of 50. This represents 50% of the total marks for the whole examination.

Preparing for the Reading section

To prepare for the Reading section, you should read the type of English used in everyday life; for example, short newspaper and magazine articles, advertisements, tourist brochures, instructions and recipes, etc. It is also a good idea to practise reading short communicative messages, including notes, emails and cards. Remember, you won't always need to understand every word to be able to do a task in the exam.

Before the exam, think about the time you need to do each part and check you know how to record your answers on the answer sheet (see page 104).

Part	Task type and format	Task focus	Number of questions
1	Matching. Matching five prompt sentences to eight notices, plus an example.	Gist understanding of real-world notices. Reading for main message.	5
2	Three-option multiple choice. Five sentences (plus an integrated example) with connecting link of topic or storyline.	Reading and identifying appropriate vocabulary.	5

3	Three-option multiple choice. Five discrete three-option multiple-choice items (plus an example) focusing on verbal exchange patterns. **AND** Matching. Five matching items (plus an example) in a continuous dialogue, selecting from eight possible responses.	Functional language. Reading and identifying the appropriate response.	10
4	Right/Wrong/Doesn't say **OR** Three-option multiple choice. One long text or three short texts adapted from authentic newspaper or magazine articles. Seven three-option multiple-choice items or Right/Wrong/ Doesn't say items, plus an example.	Reading for detailed understanding and main idea(s).	7
5	Multiple-choice cloze. A text adapted from an original source, for example an encyclopaedia entry, newspaper or magazine article. Eight three-option multiple-choice items, plus an integrated example.	Reading and identifying appropriate structural words (auxiliary verbs, modal verbs, determiners, pronouns, prepositions, conjunctions, etc.).	8

Preparing for the Writing section

To prepare for the Writing section, you should take the opportunity to write short messages in real-life situations, for example to your teacher or other students. These can include invitations, arrangements for meetings, apologies for missing a class, or notices about lost property. They can be handwritten or sent as email.

Before the exam, think about the time you need to do each part and check you know how to record your answers on the answer sheet (see page 105).

Part	Task type and format	Task focus	Number of questions
6	Word completion. Five dictionary definition type sentences (plus an example). Five words to identify and spell.	Reading and identifying appropriate vocabulary, and spelling.	5
7	Open cloze. Text type that candidates can be expected to write, for example a short letter or email. Ten spaces to fill with one word which must be spelled correctly, (plus an integrated example).	Reading and identifying appropriate words, with a focus on structure and/or vocabulary.	10
8	Information transfer. Two short authentic texts (emails, adverts, etc.) to prompt completion of another text (form, note, etc.). Five spaces to fill with one or more words or numbers (plus an integrated example).	Reading and writing appropriate words or numbers, with a focus on content and accuracy.	5
9	Guided writing. Either a short input text or a rubric to prompt a written response. Three messages to communicate in writing.	Writing a short message, note, email or postcard of 25–35 words.	1

Part 6

This part is about vocabulary. You have to produce words and spell them correctly. The words will all be linked to the same topic, for example jobs or food. You have to read a definition for each one and complete the word. The first letter of each word is given to help you.

Part 7

This part is about grammar and vocabulary. You have to complete a short, gapped text of the type you could be expected to write, such as a note, email or short letter. You must spell all the missing words correctly.

Part 8

This part tests both reading and writing. You have to use the information in two short texts (for example a note, email or advertisement) to complete a document such as a form, notice or diary entry. You will need to understand the vocabulary used on forms, for example *name*, *cost* and *time*. You will need to write only words or phrases in your answers, but you must spell them correctly.

Part 9

You have to write a short message (25–35 words). You are told who you are writing to and why, and you must include three pieces of information. To gain top marks, all three parts of the message must be included in your answer, so it is important to read the question carefully and plan what you are going to write. Before the exam, practise writing answers of the correct length. You will lose marks for writing fewer than 25 words, and it is not a good idea to write answers that are too long.

Mark Scheme for Part 9

There are five marks for Part 9. Minor grammatical and spelling mistakes are acceptable, but to get five marks you must write a clear message and include all three pieces of information.

Mark	Criteria	
5	All three parts of the message clearly communicated.	
	Only minor spelling errors or occasional grammatical errors.	
4	All three parts of the message communicated.	
	Some non-impeding errors in spelling and grammar or some awkwardness of expression.	
3	All three parts of the message attempted.	Two parts of the message clearly communicated.
	Expression requires interpretation by the reader and contains impeding errors in spelling and grammar.	Only minor spelling errors or occasional grammatical errors.
2	Only two parts of the message communicated.	
	Some errors in spelling and grammar.	
	The errors in expression may require patience and interpretation by the reader and impede communication.	
1	Only one part of the message communicated.	
0	Question unattempted, or totally incomprehensible response.	

Paper 2   Listening

Paper format
This paper contains five parts.

Number of questions
25

Task types
Matching, multiple choice, gap-fill.

Sources
All texts are based on authentic situations, and each part is heard twice.

Answering
Candidates indicate answers either by shading lozenges (Parts 1–3) or by writing answers (Parts 4 and 5) on an answer sheet.

Timing
About 30 minutes, including 8 minutes to transfer answers.

Marks
Each item carries one mark. This gives a total of 25 marks, which represents 25% of the total marks for the examination.

Preparing for the Listening test

The best preparation for the Listening test is to listen to authentic spoken English for your level. Apart from in class, other sources of English include films, TV, DVDs, songs, the internet, English clubs, and other speakers of English such as tourists, guides, friends and family.

You will hear the instructions for each task on the recording and see them on the exam paper. There are pauses in the recording to give you time to look at the questions and to write your answers. You should write your answers on the exam paper as you listen. You will have eight minutes at the end of the test to transfer your answers to the answer sheet (see page 106). Make sure you know how to do this and that you check your answers carefully.

Part	Task type and format	Task focus	Number of questions
1	Three-option multiple choice. Short, neutral or informal dialogues. Five discrete three-option multiple-choice items with pictures (plus an example).	Listening to identify key information (times, prices, days of week, numbers, etc.).	5
2	Matching. Longer informal dialogue. Five items (plus an integrated example) and eight options.	Listening to identify key information.	5
3	Three-option multiple choice. Longer informal or neutral dialogue. Five three-option multiple-choice items (plus an integrated example).	Taking the role of one of the speakers and listening to identify key information.	5
4	Gap-fill. Longer neutral or informal dialogue. Five gaps to fill with one or more words or numbers (plus an integrated example). Recognisable spelling is accepted, except with very high-frequency words (e.g. *bus*, *red*) or if spelling is dictated.	Listening and writing down information (including spelling of names, places, etc. as dictated on recording).	5
5	Gap-fill. Longer neutral or informal monologue. Five gaps to fill with one or more words or numbers (plus an integrated example). Recognisable spelling is accepted, except with very high-frequency words (e.g. *bus*, *red*) or if spelling is dictated.	Listening and writing down information (including spelling of names, places, etc. as dictated on recording).	5

Paper 3   Speaking

Paper format

The paper contains two parts. The standard format for Paper 3 is two candidates and two examiners. One examiner acts only as an assessor and does not join in the conversation. The other examiner is called the interlocutor and manages the interaction by asking questions and setting up the tasks.

Task types

Short exchanges with the interlocutor and an interactive task involving both candidates.

Timing

8–10 minutes per pair of candidates.

Marks

Candidates are assessed on their performance throughout the test. There are a total of 25 marks, making 25% of the total score for the whole examination.

Preparing for the Speaking test

Take every opportunity to practise your English with as many people as possible. Asking and answering questions in simple role plays provides useful practice. These role plays should focus on everyday language and situations, and involve questions about daily activities and familiar experiences. It is also a good idea to practise exchanging information in role plays about things such as the costs and opening times of, for example, a local sports centre.

Part	Task type and format	Task focus	Timing
1	Each candidate interacts with the interlocutor. The interlocutor asks the candidates questions. The interlocutor follows an interlocutor frame to guide the conversation, ensure standardisation, and control the level of input.	Language normally associated with meeting people for the first time, giving information of a factual, personal kind. Bio-data type questions to respond to.	5–6 minutes
2	Candidates interact with each other. The interlocutor sets up the activity using a standardised rubric. Candidates ask and answer questions using prompt material.	Factual information of a non-personal kind related to daily life.	3–4 minutes

Assessment

Throughout the Speaking test the examiners listen to what you say and give you marks for how well you speak English, so you must try to speak about the tasks and answer the examiner's and your partner's questions.

The two examiners mark different aspects of your speaking. One of the examiners (the assessor) will give marks on the following:

Grammar and Vocabulary

This refers to the range of language you use and also how accurately you use grammar and vocabulary.

Pronunciation

This refers to how easy it is to understand what you say. You should be able to say words and sentences that are easy to understand.

Interactive Communication

This refers to how well you can talk about a task, and to your partner and the examiner, and whether you can ask for repetition or clarification if needed.

Band	Grammar and Vocabulary	Pronunciation	Interactive Communication
5	• Shows a good degree of control of simple grammatical forms. • Uses a range of appropriate vocabulary when talking about everyday situations.	• Is mostly intelligible, and has some control of phonological features at both utterance and word levels.	• Maintains simple exchanges. • Requires very little prompting and support.
4	*Performance shares features of Bands 3 and 5.*		
3	• Shows sufficient control of simple grammatical forms. • Uses appropriate vocabulary to talk about everyday situations.	• Is mostly intelligible, despite limited control of phonological features.	• Maintains simple exchanges, despite some difficulty. • Requires prompting and support.
2	*Performance shares features of Bands 1 and 3.*		
1	• Shows only limited control of a few grammatical forms. • Uses a vocabulary of isolated words and phrases.	• Has very limited control of phonological features and is often unintelligible.	• Has considerable difficulty maintaining simple exchanges. • Requires additional prompting and support.
0	*Performance below Band 1.*		

The examiner asking the questions (the interlocutor) gives marks for how well you do overall, using a Global Achievement scale.

Band	Global Achievement
5	• Handles communication in everyday situations, despite hesitation. • Constructs longer utterances but is not able to use complex language except in well-rehearsed utterances.
4	*Performance shares features of Bands 3 and 5.*
3	• Conveys basic meaning in very familiar everyday situations. • Produces utterances which tend to be very short – words or phrases – with frequent hesitation and pauses.
2	*Performance shares features of Bands 1 and 3.*
1	• Has difficulty conveying basic meaning even in very familiar everyday situations. • Responses are limited to short phrases or isolated words with frequent hesitation and pauses.
0	*Performance below Band 1.*

Further information

The information in this practice book is designed to give an overview of *Cambridge English: Key*. For a full description of all the *Cambridge English* exams, including information about task types, testing focus and preparation, please see the relevant handbooks which can be obtained from Cambridge ESOL at the address below or from the website: www.CambridgeESOL.org.

University of Cambridge
ESOL Examinations
1 Hills Road
Cambridge
CB1 2EU
United Kingdom

Telephone: +44 1223 553997
Fax: +44 1223 553621
Email: ESOLHelpdesk@CambridgeESOL.org

Test 1

PAPER 1   READING AND WRITING (1 hour 10 minutes)

PART 1

QUESTIONS 1–5

Which notice (A–H) says this (1–5)?
For questions 1–5, mark the correct letter A–H on your answer sheet.

Example:

0   You can buy photographs in this shop that
were taken by someone who lives nearby.

Answer:

0	A	B	C	D	E	F	G	H
	☐	☐	☐	☐	■	☐	☐	☐

---

1   You can learn how to paint here.

    A
> Passport photographs
> are ready in 5 minutes

2   If you go shopping here this week, you'll
pay much less than usual.

    B
> Monica's art class will
> be in room 31 today

    C
> City Museum
> Talk on 16th-century artists
> Wednesday, 6.30 pm   £2

3   This place is not open every day.

    D
> The Art Centre library is
> now closed on Fridays

4   You won't have to wait long before you
get your pictures.

    E
> Winton Stores
> Postcards by our village
> photographer on sale inside

    F
> Homestore
> all paint half-price – for one month only

5   Someone has just painted a door in this
building.

    G
> Wet Paint!
> Please use other entrance

    H
> Burley Art Club
> Sale of paintings starts Monday

PART 2

QUESTIONS 6–10

Read the sentences about camping.
Choose the best word (A, B or C) for each space.
For questions 6–10, mark A, B or C on your answer sheet.

Example:

0   A lot of families prefer to .... on a campsite because it is cheaper than a hotel.

   A   keep   **B**   stay   **C**   travel   *Answer:* | 0 | A B C ☐ ■ ☐ |

---

6   For some campsites, you have to phone and .... before you go.

   A   book   **B**   take   **C**   spend

7   Some people play loud music on campsites so it can be very ....

   A   angry   **B**   busy   **C**   noisy

8   One of the nicest things about camping is .... breakfast outside.

   A   doing   **B**   having   **C**   putting

9   It is better to use plastic cups and plates for camping because they don't .... easily.

   A   break   **B**   hurt   **C**   fail

10   One problem with camping is making .... insects don't get into the tent.

   A   careful   **B**   clear   **C**   sure

PART 3

QUESTIONS 11–15

Complete the five conversations.
For questions 11–15, mark A, B or C on your answer sheet.

Example:

0

Where do you come from?

A New York.

B School.

C Home.

Answer:

---

11 Is it a good film?

    A That's right.

    B It's OK.

    C I don't agree.

12 I'm going to Tom's party tonight.

    A Can I go too?

    B Let's go.

    C Was it good?

13 When did you lose your watch?

    A Once a week.

    B For six days.

    C A month ago.

14 Sorry, I don't understand you.

    A Let me explain.

    B I don't know.

    C What does it mean?

15 Shall we ask Paul to come with us?

    A I believe it.

    B I'm sure.

    C If you like.

QUESTIONS 16–20

Complete the telephone conversation between two friends.
What does Jennifer say to Lily?
For questions 16–20, mark the correct letter A–H on your answer sheet.

Example:

Lily: Hi Jennifer, it will be lovely to see you on Friday.

Jennifer: 0 ....**B**............

Answer: | 0 | A B C D E F G H |

Lily: What time is your train?

Jennifer: 16 ....

Lily: OK. I'll meet you. Would you like to go out that evening?

Jennifer: 17 ....

Lily: If you want to. Then on Saturday we can go to the new shopping centre.

Jennifer: 18 ....

Lily: And in the evening we can go to Oliver's party.

Jennifer: 19 ....

Lily: Oh anything. It doesn't matter.

Jennifer: 20 ....

Lily: Yes. It's a good place for a party. See you Friday, then.

A I have to go home at 6 o'clock.

B Yes, I haven't seen you for so long.

C I've heard it's really big.

D Is he still living in the same house?

E It should arrive early afternoon.

F How long will we stay with him there?

G I think I'll be tired. Shall we just stay at home?

H Great! What should I bring to wear?

PART 4

QUESTIONS 21–27

Read the article about a man who swam across New Zealand's Cook Strait.
Are sentences 21–27 'Right' (A) or 'Wrong' (B)?
If there is not enough information to answer 'Right' (A) or 'Wrong' (B), choose
'Doesn't say' (C).
For questions 21–27, mark A, B or C on your answer sheet.

David swims the Cook Strait

David Johnson has loved swimming all his life. When he was 27, he swam in a race near his home in the USA. The sea was very cold and David started to feel unwell. He was taken to hospital but he soon got better and started swimming again. In 1983, he became the first person to swim from Santa Cruz Island to the Californian coast.

In January 2004, at the age of 52, David crossed New Zealand's Cook Strait in 9 hours and 38 minutes. The oldest swimmer before David was only 42 years old. David spent over a year getting ready to swim the Strait. Then, he and his wife flew to New Zealand so that David could practise for a few weeks there. But, only days after they arrived, the weather improved so David decided to start his swim. He did it with the help of a team. 'They were great,' David said. 'They were in a boat next to me all the time! After a few hours, I thought about stopping but I didn't and went on swimming.'

Afterwards, David and his wife travelled around New Zealand before returning to the USA.

Example:

0   David Johnson has always enjoyed swimming.

   A Right   **B** Wrong   **C** Doesn't say   *Answer:* | 0 | A ■ | B ☐ | C ☐ |

---

21   David Johnson had problems during a swimming competition in the USA.

   A Right   **B** Wrong   **C** Doesn't say

22   After 1983, many people swam between Santa Cruz Island and the Californian coast.

   A Right   **B** Wrong   **C** Doesn't say

23   In January 2004, David was the first person of his age to swim across the Cook Strait.

   A Right   **B** Wrong   **C** Doesn't say

24   David practised for more than a year to swim across the Cook Strait.

   A Right   **B** Wrong   **C** Doesn't say

25   David was in New Zealand for a long time before he swam across the Cook Strait.

   A Right   **B** Wrong   **C** Doesn't say

26   David's wife was in the boat beside him when he swam the Cook Strait.

   A Right   **B** Wrong   **C** Doesn't say

27   David had to stop for a short time while swimming the Cook Strait.

   A Right   **B** Wrong   **C** Doesn't say

PART 5

QUESTIONS 28–35

Read the article about doing homework.
Choose the best word (A, B or C) for each space.
For questions 28–35, mark A, B or C on your answer sheet.

Doing homework

It is a good idea to **(0)** .... your homework early. If you can do it **(28)** .... your evening meal, you will have **(29)** .... time later to do things that you enjoy, like talking **(30)** .... the phone.

It is also better to do homework as soon as possible after the teacher has given it to you. Then, if the homework is difficult and you **(31)** .... time to think about it, you will **(32)** .... have time to do it.

Always turn off your mobile phone and the television when you **(33)** .... doing homework. You will work a lot **(34)** .... without them. Make sure you have a quiet place to work, with **(35)** .... light and a comfortable chair.

Example:

0   **A** starting   **B** started   **C** start   *Answer:* [0] [A B C ▢▢■]

---

28   **A** since   **B** before   **C** until

29   **A** more   **B** much   **C** most

30   **A** by   **B** at   **C** on

31   **A** should   **B** need   **C** must

32   **A** still   **B** yet   **C** already

33   **A** have   **B** are   **C** were

34   **A** fastest   **B** fast   **C** faster

35   **A** enough   **B** all   **C** many

PART 6

QUESTIONS 36–40

Read the descriptions of some things you can find in a kitchen.
What is the word for each one?
The first letter is already there. There is one space for each other letter in the word.
For questions 36–40, write the words on your answer sheet.

Example:

0 Breakfast, lunch and dinner are all examples of this.   m _ _ _

Answer:

0	m e a l

---

36 This keeps food and drink cold.   f _ _ _ _ _

37 You use this to cut things.   k _ _ _ _

38 You do this to water to make it hot enough for a cup of coffee.   b _ _ _

39 Some people put this in their drinks to make them sweet.   s _ _ _ _

40 You can make chips with this vegetable.   p _ _ _ _ _

PART 7

QUESTIONS 41–50

Complete the letter.
Write ONE word for each space.
For questions 41–50, write the words on your answer sheet.

Example: | **0** | f o r |

Dear Giulia,

Thank you **(0)** .... the lovely birthday present. I already had some CDs by the same singer but I didn't have **(41)** .... one. I like it **(42)** .... much.

I **(43)** .... a lovely time on my birthday. My parents took me **(44)** .... a Japanese restaurant for lunch. The food was excellent and **(45)** .... all enjoyed it. **(46)** .... were some famous actors sitting near to **(47)** .... table. I asked **(48)** .... to write their names on my menu. They wrote: 'To Sunniya with love on your birthday'. It was **(49)** .... great day. I'll **(50)** .... forget meeting them.

Love,

Sunniya

PART 8

QUESTIONS 51–55

Read the advertisement and the email.

Fill in the information in Anna's notes.

For questions 51–55, write the information on your answer sheet.

Cinemax Cinema **Monday 8 – Sunday 14 June** **BLUE JUICE** 4.30 pm | 7.15 pm | 8.30 pm **Moon Race** 3.45 pm | 8.45 pm Tickets: £4.75 £5.50 for films after 6 pm	**From:** Jed **To:** Anna Can you book our tickets? I'm working Friday evening but can go on Saturday. I don't want to see Blue Juice – I think the other film is better. Shall we go at the later time? Then we can eat before it starts. I'll wait for you in the café opposite at 7.30.

Anna's notes
Cinema visit

Name of cinema:	Cinemax
Name of film:	**51**
Day:	**52**
Start time:	**53** _____ pm
Cost per person:	**54** £
Place to meet Jed:	**55**

PART 9

QUESTION 56

Your friend Sam is coming to your house tomorrow evening.
Write a note to Sam.

Tell Sam:

- **what** time to come

- **what** to bring

- **how** to get to your house.

Write 25–35 words.
Write the note on your answer sheet.

PAPER 2 LISTENING (approximately 30 minutes including 8 minutes transfer time)

PART 1

QUESTIONS 1–5

You will hear five short conversations.
You will hear each conversation twice.
There is one question for each conversation.
For questions 1–5, put a tick (✓) under the right answer.

Example:

0 How many people were at the meeting?

3	13	30
☐	☐	☑

---

1 What must the man turn off?

☐ ☐ ☐

2 Where's the girl's pen?

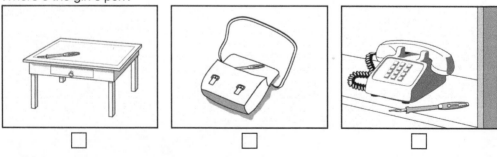

☐ ☐ ☐

3   What will the boy do this evening?

☐   ☐   ☐

4   What animals did they see on their holiday?

☐   ☐   ☐

5   What does the man want to buy?

      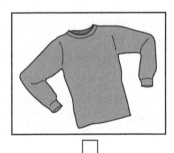

☐   ☐   ☐

PART 2

QUESTIONS 6–10

Listen to David and Eva talking about a school art lesson.
Where did they and their friends go to draw their pictures?
For questions 6–10, write a letter A–H next to each person.
You will hear the conversation twice.

Example:

0   David   E

People

6   Eva

7   Luke

8   Mary

9   Patrick

10   Cristina

Places

A   bank

B   café

C   castle

D   market

E   museum

F   park

G   river

H   swimming pool

PART 3

QUESTIONS 11–15

Listen to Dawn talking about her trip to California.
For questions 11–15, tick (✓) A, B or C.
You will hear the conversation twice.

Example:

0	Dawn went to California	A	last week.	☐
		B	last month.	✓
		C	last year.	☐

11	Dawn booked the concert ticket	A	on the internet.	☐
		B	over the phone.	☐
		C	by post.	☐

12	Dawn's plane ticket cost	A	£230.	☐
		B	£300.	☐
		C	£350.	☐

13	Dawn stayed in	A	a student hotel.	☐
		B	a family friend's home.	☐
		C	a campsite.	☐

14 Dawn thought the concert was

A not very good. ☐

B too short. ☐

C too noisy. ☐

15 Most of the time, Dawn was

A on the beach. ☐

B on a tour bus. ☐

C in the shops. ☐

PART 4

QUESTIONS 16–20

You will hear André telling a friend about his tennis lessons.
Listen and complete questions 16–20.
You will hear the conversation twice.

André's tennis lessons

Teacher's name:	Paul
Day:	**16**
Cost:	**17** £ .... per hour
At tennis courts in:	**18** .... Street
Starting time:	**19** .... pm
Wear:	**20** .... and T-shirt

PART 5

QUESTIONS 21–25

You will hear someone talking on the radio about a hotel in Ireland.
Listen and complete questions 21–25.
You will hear the information twice.

Hotel in Ireland

Best time to visit: June

Name: **21** The .... Hotel

Where: **22** .... Island

Hotel first built in the year: **23**

Number of bedrooms: **24**

Restaurant famous for: **25**

You now have 8 minutes to write your answers on the answer sheet.

PAPER 3 SPEAKING (8–10 minutes)

The Speaking test lasts 8 to 10 minutes. You will take the test with another candidate. There are two examiners, but only one of them will talk to you. The examiner will ask you questions and ask you to talk to the other candidate.

Part 1 (5–6 minutes)

The examiner will ask you and your partner some questions. These questions will be about your daily life, past experience and future plans. For example, you may have to speak about your school, job, hobbies or home town.

Part 2 (3–4 minutes)

You and your partner will speak to each other. You will ask and answer questions. The examiner will give you a card with some information on it. The examiner will give your partner a card with some words on it. Your partner will use the words on the card to ask you questions about the information you have. Then you will change roles.

Test 2

PAPER 1 READING AND WRITING (1 hour 10 minutes)

PART 1

QUESTIONS 1–5

Which notice (A–H) says this (1–5)?
For questions 1–5, mark the correct letter A–H on your answer sheet.

Example:

0 You must not take photographs in here.

Answer:

0	A	B	C	D	E	F	G	H
	☐	☐	☐	☐	☐	☐	☐	■

---

1 Do not leave any food here.

A
> School Trip to the Sea
> *Don't forget your picnic!*

2 Do not leave your suitcases in front of the doors.

B
> **City Airport**
> Please keep exits free from luggage

C
> **INGHAM COUNTRY PARK**
> After eating, take your picnic things home

3 You can write to people from here.

D
> Please write your name and address on all your suitcases

4 Do not bring your own sandwiches here.

E
> *Internet Café*
> *Send emails, surf the net*
> *£2 per hour*

5 Be very careful to watch your bags and suitcases.

F
> **Central Station**
> Keep your luggage with you at all times

G
> Pietro's Café
> Please only eat food you have bought here

H
> **SOUTHPORT ART MUSEUM**
> Sorry, <u>no</u> cameras

PART 2

QUESTIONS 6–10

Read the sentences about Ingrid's home.
Choose the best word (A, B or C) for each space.
For questions 6–10, mark A, B or C on your
answer sheet.

Example:

0   Ingrid lives in a flat on the seventh .... of a large, modern building.

    A   floor   **B**   line   **C**   platform   *Answer:*

0	A	B	C
	■	☐	☐

---

6   Ingrid likes living .... above the city streets.

    A   tall   **B**   high   **C**   long

7   Ingrid was born in the countryside, but she .... living in the city.

    A   hopes   **B**   wants   **C**   prefers

8   It only .... Ingrid ten minutes to walk from the flat to her school.

    A   uses   **B**   takes   **C**   needs

9   When the lift isn't .... Ingrid has to walk up the stairs to her flat!

    A   arriving   **B**   climbing   **C**   working

10   When she gets home, her mother cooks a big ....

    A   meal   **B**   dish   **C**   food

PART 3

QUESTIONS 11–15

Complete the five conversations.

For questions 11–15, mark A, B or C on your answer sheet.

Example:

0

Where do you come from?

A New York.

B School.

C Home.

Answer: 0 [A ■] [B □] [C □]

---

11 I like your new dress.

A Do you really?

B What's it like?

C Do you think so?

12 How did you get to Portugal?

A It was £50.

B Last week.

C By plane.

13 I'm sorry I'm late.

A You can't go.

B That's all right.

C There isn't time.

14 Hello. Can I speak to Jane, please?

A Can I leave a message?

B I'll try again later.

C Can I ask who's calling?

15 Remember to buy some coffee!

A I won't forget.

B I don't mind.

C I'm certain, thank you.

QUESTIONS 16–20

Complete the conversation.

What does Sara say to her father?

For questions 16–20, mark the correct letter A–H on your answer sheet.

Example:

Father: Hi Sara. Did you have a good day at school?

Sara: 0 ....**G**............

Answer: | 0 | A B C D E F G H |

Father:	Good, thanks. I played a game of golf.	**A**	Our teacher said we needed it – but it was so boring.
Sara:	16	**B**	OK. But why don't we play today?
Father:	Oh! Why was that?		
Sara:	17	**C**	Where did you play?
Father:	Oh well. Did you play tennis this afternoon?	**D**	Mm, I should do my homework first. Let's go later.
Sara:	18	**E**	You're lucky! We had an extra maths lesson.
Father:	Good for you! We must have a game at the weekend.	**F**	I did. It was really good. I won all my games!
Sara:	19		
Father:	Good idea. Would you like to go now?	**G**	Not bad. How was your day?
Sara:	20	**H**	Then we can have dinner after our game.
Father:	OK. Dinner will be ready at 7, so we can go at about 8.		

PART 4

QUESTIONS 21–27

Read the article about two strange meetings.
Are sentences 21–27 'Right' (A) or 'Wrong' (B)?
If there is not enough information to answer 'Right' (A) or 'Wrong' (B), choose
'Doesn't say' (C).
For questions 21–27, mark A, B or C on your answer sheet.

We meet twice

My name is Anna King and I was born in a small town called Madison in Wyoming in the centre of the USA. When I was twenty, I moved to the east coast, to a town just south of New York, to start a job in a department store. One day, a young man with short brown hair who was shopping in the store looked at me and asked, 'Are you Michelle Golden?'

'No,' I said. 'But do you mean Michelle Golden from Madison?' He did. I told him that I was at school with Michelle. She wasn't much older than me and people often said that we looked just like each other. Then the young man told me that Michelle was in the same history class at university as he was.

Six months later, I got a better job with another department store and moved to the west coast to work at their San Francisco store. One day on my way home from work, a young man with short brown hair passed me in the street and asked, 'Are you Michelle Golden?'

'No,' I answered. 'You asked me that when we met in a shop several thousand miles away, near New York.'

Example:

0   Anna was born in a large town.

A   Right   **B**   Wrong   **C**   Doesn't say

Answer:

---

21   Anna left home and began working in a department store.

A   Right   **B**   Wrong   **C**   Doesn't say

22   The young man who spoke to Anna wanted to buy a new jacket.

A   Right   **B**   Wrong   **C**   Doesn't say

23   Anna was younger than Michelle.

A   Right   **B**   Wrong   **C**   Doesn't say

24   Michelle and the young man were students together.

A   Right   **B**   Wrong   **C**   Doesn't say

25   Anna got a job with the same company in San Francisco.

A   Right   **B**   Wrong   **C**   Doesn't say

26   Anna was at work when she met the young man for the second time.

A   Right   **B**   Wrong   **C**   Doesn't say

27   Anna was angry when the young man spoke to her a second time.

A   Right   **B**   Wrong   **C**   Doesn't say

PART 5

QUESTIONS 28–35

Read the article about tigers.

Choose the best word (**A, B** or **C**) for each space.

For questions **28–35**, mark **A, B** or **C** on your answer sheet.

Tigers

Tigers are the **(0)** .... cats of all. A hundred years ago 100,000 tigers lived across Asia, but today **(28)** .... are only about 6000, with **(29)** .... living in zoos around the world.

Tigers usually live in forests but **(30)** .... are found in wetter areas. Most of them live **(31)** .... 12 to 18 years, but in zoos they can live **(32)** .... they are 25. The coats of **(33)** .... beautiful animals are orange and black but, surprisingly, no two coats are ever the **(34)** .... They look for food at night, and will eat fish and birds as well as larger animals.

Tigers are different from most cats because they like water. They are strong swimmers, and often go into rivers when the weather gets **(35)** .... hot.

Example:

| 0 | A | large | B | larger | C | largest | *Answer:* | 0 | A B C ☐☐■ |

---

28 A that   B it   C there

29 A much   B many   C any

30 A each   B every   C some

31 A from   B in   C through

32 A during   B until   C above

33 A these   B those   C this

34 A same   B one   C other

35 A such   B too   C enough

PART 6

QUESTIONS 36–40

Read the descriptions of some things people often carry with them in their bags or pockets.

What is the word for each one?

The first letter is already there. There is one space for each other letter in the word.

For questions 36–40, write the words on your answer sheet.

Example:

0   If you drive a car, you should carry this with you.   l __ __ __ __ __ __

Answer: | **0** | *licence* |

---

36   People often write their appointments in this.   d __ __ __ __ __

37   Some people wear these so they can see better.   g __ __ __ __ __ __ __

38   You will need to keep this with you when you travel by train.   t __ __ __ __ __ __

39   You can read about famous people in this and it also
         has lots of pictures.   m __ __ __ __ __ __ __ __

40   Many people keep their money inside this.   w __ __ __ __ __ __

PART 7

QUESTIONS 41–50

Complete the email.
Write **ONE** word for each space.
For questions 41–50, write the words on your answer sheet.

Example: | **0** | *f o r* |
|---|---|

From:	Margaret
To:	Lidija

Thank you **(0)** .... letting me stay **(41)** .... you in Ljubljana last week. Slovenia's a great country and **(42)** .... was really nice to spend a **(43)** .... days with you and your family. I learned so **(44)** .... about Slovenian cooking from your mother!

I really enjoyed meeting your friends **(45)** .... the university too. Please say hello to all of **(46)** ....

I **(47)** .... like to come back to Slovenia. If I do that, I'll make sure I can speak more **(48)** .... your language. What **(49)** .... the best Slovene textbook?

I **(50)** .... everyone in your family is well.

PART 8

QUESTIONS 51–55

Read the advertisement and the email.

Fill in the information in Marco's notes.

For questions 51–55, write the information on your answer sheet.

CAMP BELLAMY

SPRING ACTIVITIES

Climbing	**Sailing**
(Ages 13–16)	(Ages 17–19)
£60	£80

Times: 8.30 am or 2.30 pm

Courses begin:
14 April and 21 April

From: Connor

To: Marco

I've booked us on the climbing course in the afternoon at Camp Bellamy because we're not old enough to go sailing.

I know you're on holiday until 15 April, so we will start on 21 April. You need to bring some food with you but we are given special shoes when we arrive.

Marco's notes
Spring activities

Name of camp:	Camp Bellamy
Activity booked:	51
Start date:	52
Time:	53
Price per person:	54 £
Take:	55

PART 9

QUESTION 56

You have just started a new summer job.
Write an email to your English friend, Pat.

Say:

- **what** your new job is

- **which days** you work

- **why** you like it.

Write 25–35 words.
Write the email on your answer sheet.

PAPER 2   LISTENING (approximately 30 minutes including 8 minutes transfer time)

PART 1

QUESTIONS 1–5

You will hear five short conversations.
You will hear each conversation twice.
There is one question for each conversation.
For questions 1–5, put a tick (✓) under the right answer.

Example:

0   How many people were at the meeting?

3	13	30
☐	☐	✓

---

1   Which day is the man's appointment?

Thursday	Friday	Monday
☐	☐	☐

2   What is the woman going to eat?

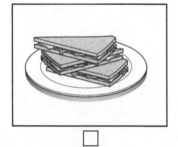  

☐	☐	☐

3   Which train will the woman take?

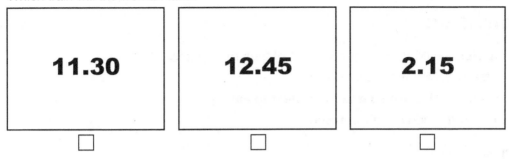

4   How much did the man pay for the camera?

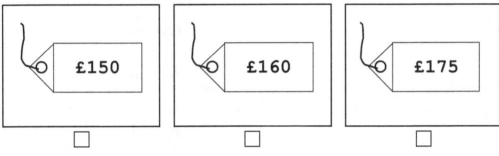

5   Which race did the girl win?

PART 2

QUESTIONS 6–10

Listen to Rosie talking to a friend about places for a party.
What is the problem with each place?
For questions 6–10, write a letter A–H next to each place.
You will hear the conversation twice.

Example:

0	University Hotel	**G**

Places			**Problems**	
6	Brown's Café		**A**	closed
			B	cold
7	Rivers Hotel		**C**	dark
8	Bridge Restaurant		**D**	dirty
			E	expensive
9	Garden House		**F**	full
			G	old
10	Opera Café		**H**	small

PART 3

QUESTIONS 11–15

Listen to Joe asking about a French language course.
For questions 11–15, tick (✓) A, B or C.
You will hear the conversation twice.

Example:

0	Lessons for beginners are on	**A**	Monday.	☐
		B	Wednesday.	✓
		C	Friday.	☐

11	The best class for Joe is	**A**	French Conversation.	☐
		B	Business French.	☐
		C	French for Tourists.	☐

12	Joe's class begins at	**A**	6.30.	☐
		B	7.15.	☐
		C	8.30.	☐

13	How many other students will there be in Joe's class?	**A**	9	☐
		B	14	☐
		C	15	☐

14 What should Joe take to his first class?

    A a dictionary ☐

    B a coursebook ☐

    C a notebook ☐

15 Joe will pay

    A £25. ☐

    B £145. ☐

    C £170. ☐

PART 4

QUESTIONS 16–20

You will hear a girl asking for information about going to Kendal by bus.
Listen and complete questions 16–20.
You will hear the conversation twice.

Bus to Kendal

First bus leaves at:	6.45 am
Cost of single ticket:	**16** £
Buy ticket from:	**17**
Address of bus station:	**18** .... Street
next to:	**19**
At bus station, you can buy:	**20** .... and newspapers

PART 5

QUESTIONS 21–25

You will hear a telephone message about a trip to the theatre.
Listen and complete questions 21–25.
You will hear the information twice.

☎ **Telephone message** ☎

To: Jamie

From: Michael

Name of play: **21** The .... Party

Date: **22** .... August

The theatre is opposite: **23** the ....

Meet Michael at: **24** .... pm

Mobile number: **25**

You now have 8 minutes to write your answers on the answer sheet.

PAPER 3 SPEAKING (8–10 minutes)

The Speaking test lasts 8 to 10 minutes. You will take the test with another candidate. There are two examiners, but only one of them will talk to you. The examiner will ask you questions and ask you to talk to the other candidate.

Part 1 (5–6 minutes)

The examiner will ask you and your partner some questions. These questions will be about your daily life, past experience and future plans. For example, you may have to speak about your school, job, hobbies or home town.

Part 2 (3–4 minutes)

You and your partner will speak to each other. You will ask and answer questions. The examiner will give you a card with some information on it. The examiner will give your partner a card with some words on it. Your partner will use the words on the card to ask you questions about the information you have. Then you will change roles.

Test 3

PAPER 1   READING AND WRITING (1 hour 10 minutes)

PART 1

QUESTIONS 1–5

Which notice (A–H) says this (1–5)?
For questions 1–5, mark the correct letter A–H on your answer sheet.

Example:

0   You can leave your luggage here.

Answer:

0	A	B	C	D	E	F	G	H
	☐	☐	☐	☐	■	☐	☐	☐

---

1   Some lorries cannot go under this.

A
> **Western Railway**
> **Woodville Town – Drayton Park**
> **Monday – Friday only**

2   You cannot travel by these trains at the weekend.

B
> **Bus to City Centre**
> **Adults £1.50**
> **Children under 2 travel free**

C
> **ALL DRIVERS!**
> **BRIDGE ONLY 5 METRES HIGH**

3   You must pay to leave your car here.

D
> **Airport Bus**
> **5 am – 11.30 pm daily**
> **£11 return**

4   Use this if you have to catch a plane.

E
> **City Trains**
> **Please put large bags between seats**

F
> **Hospital Parking**
> **for visitors**
> **£2 per hour**

5   You may sit where you like.

G
> **Choose any seat on the plane**
> **No numbers on tickets**

H
> **Drive Slowly**
> **Lorries Turning**

PART 2

QUESTIONS 6–10

Read the sentences about an ice-hockey player.
Choose the best word (A, B or C) for each space.
For questions 6–10, mark A, B or C on your answer
sheet.

Example:

0   Neil .... to play ice-hockey even when he was a very small boy.

    A   enjoyed   **B**   wanted   **C**   welcomed   *Answer:*   0   A B C ☐ ■ ☐

---

6   Neil .... ice-hockey every evening with his team.

    A   made   **B**   joined   **C**   practised

7   Neil was an excellent player and his team soon began to .... competitions.

    A   earn   **B**   win   **C**   take

8   Sometimes it was .... for Neil to find enough time for both his ice-hockey and homework.

    A   difficult   **B**   terrible   **C**   worse

9   When he .... school at sixteen, Neil went to a special sports college.

    A   moved   **B**   left   **C**   passed

10   Now Neil is a famous ice-hockey player and you can often .... him on television.

    A   listen   **B**   see   **C**   look

PART 3

QUESTIONS 11–15

Complete the five conversations.
For questions 11–15, mark A, B or C on your answer sheet.

Example:

0

Where do you come from?

A New York.

B School.

C Home.

Answer:

---

11 Is there any sugar?

    A Nothing.

    B I need it.

    C I'm afraid not.

12 Let's go to the concert tonight.

    A Have you got tickets?

    B Who was playing?

    C What's it about?

13 Can you carry these bags?

    A It doesn't matter.

    B I'm fine, thanks.

    C Well, I'll try.

14 Thanks for a lovely meal.

    A I enjoyed seeing you.

    B I'll be ready soon.

    C I don't want to come.

15 How is your mother?

    A She's 54.

    B Much better, thanks.

    C She's tall and beautiful.

QUESTIONS 16–20

Complete the conversation between two friends.
What does Anita say to Ivan?
For questions 16–20, mark the correct letter A–H on your answer sheet.

Example:

Ivan:	Hi Anita. How was your weekend?		

| *Anita:* | 0 ....E................ | *Answer:* | 0 |

	A B C D E F G H

Ivan:	OK, but I had a bit of a problem on Saturday.	**A**	She'll love them.
Anita:	16	**B**	Did you want to go anywhere special?
Ivan:	In a way. I couldn't find my keys.		
Anita:	17..........................	**C**	How did they get there?
Ivan:	Only to the shops. I needed a birthday present for my mum.	**D**	Well, at least you've got them now.
Anita:	18..........................	**E**	Great, thanks. What about yours?
Ivan:	I bought some chocolates from the local shop. Do you think that'll be OK?	**F**	Did you have trouble with your car again?
Anita:	19..........................		
Ivan:	I hope so! I found my car keys this morning. They were in the bathroom.	**G**	She'll help you find them.
Anita:	20..........................	**H**	So did you get her anything in the end?
Ivan:	Yes, so I can drive you home, if you like.		

PART 4

QUESTIONS 21–27

Read the article about Ravi Patra, who works on music programmes on television, and then answer the questions.

For questions 21–27, mark A, B or C on your answer sheet.

Ravi Patra

In 2006, Ravi Patra started working for a music company and three years later, in 2009, got a job on the music television channel Rock TV.

Ravi enjoys working on television, but when he was younger he wanted to fly planes. Later, he became more interested in football. But Ravi has always loved music, so he tried to get work with Rock TV. His boss says he gave him the job because he wanted it more than anybody else!

When he started at Rock TV, Ravi arrived first at the office and was the last to leave at 10 in the evening. Now, he starts a bit later, but he is still busy until 10 pm. Before lunch, he usually writes his words for the show and in the afternoon he has meetings or makes Rock TV advertisements.

Ravi has many popular bands on his show and the stars are often interesting people. But Ravi knows that everyone watches the show to hear great music. Getting that right is more important than anything else.

Ravi knows what questions to ask the band members. He tries to make them laugh and this is easy for him. Sometimes he cannot remember their names but he always has information about the bands to help him.

Sadly, his work means that he doesn't see his friends enough, but he has great fun on skiing trips and listens to music all the time.

Example:

0	Ravi Patra started working with Rock TV in	**A**	2003.	*Answer:*	0	A B C
		B	2006.			
		C	2009.			

---

21 What was the first job Ravi wanted to have when he was younger?

    A footballer
    B pilot
    C singer

22 What did Ravi's boss at Rock TV say about him?

    A Ravi asked for a job at Rock TV more than once.
    B There were other people better than Ravi.
    C Ravi showed him how much he wanted the job.

23 How has Ravi's work changed?

    A He no longer begins very early.
    B He is busier than before.
    C He doesn't stay late at the office.

24 In the mornings, Ravi often

    A works on Rock TV advertisements.
    B meets important people at his office.
    C decides what to say on his programme.

25 What does Ravi think is the most important thing about the show?

    A It has lots of interesting stars.
    B There is great music.
    C He is popular with the guests.

26 What problem does Ravi sometimes have on the Rock TV show?

    A He forgets people's names.
    B He cannot stop laughing.
    C His questions make people angry.

27 Ravi would like to spend more time

    A in the mountains.
    B with his friends.
    C listening to music.

PART 5

QUESTIONS 28–35

Read the article about a mountain in Japan.

Choose the best word (A, B or C) for each space.

For questions 28–35, mark A, B or C on your answer sheet.

Mount Fuji

Mount Fuji is **(0)** .... Fujisan in Japan. It is 3776 metres high and is visited **(28)** .... people from all over the world. It is a very beautiful mountain and many artists have used it in **(29)** .... work.

It is sometimes possible to see Mount Fuji from Tokyo, but often the weather is **(30)** .... cloudy to see it clearly. The **(31)** .... time to see the mountain is **(32)** .... the colder months of the year, and **(33)** .... the early morning and late evening.

A very pleasant place to enjoy Mount Fuji from is Fuji Five Lake (Fujigoko), **(34)** .... is just north of the mountain. Mount Fuji is open for climbing in July and August, but not at **(35)** .... times of the year.

Example:

0	**A** called	**B** calling	**C** calls	*Answer:*

28	**A** by	**B** for	**C** with
29	**A** his	**B** your	**C** their
30	**A** too	**B** very	**C** only
31	**A** good	**B** better	**C** best
32	**A** since	**B** during	**C** until
33	**A** on	**B** in	**C** at
34	**A** which	**B** what	**C** where
35	**A** another	**B** both	**C** other

PART 6

QUESTIONS 36–40

Read the descriptions of some things in a bathroom.
What is the word for each one?
The first letter is already there. There is one space for each other letter in the word.
For questions 36–40, write the words on your answer sheet.

Example:

0   You can use this to tidy your hair.   c __ __ __

Answer: | **0** | c o m b |

---

36   People stand under this to wash themselves.   s __ __ __ __ __

37   If this is large, the bathroom will have lots of light
when it is sunny.   w __ __ __ __ __

38   People wash their hair with this.   s __ __ __ __ __ __

39   You can look at yourself in this.   m __ __ __ __ __

40   If your hands are dirty, you can wash them with this. s __ __ __

PART 7

QUESTIONS 41–50

Complete the emails.
Write ONE word for each space.
For questions 41–50, write the words on your answer sheet.

Example: | **0** | *y o u* |

From:	Danny
To:	Ali

I heard that **(0)** .... want to sell your bike.

Is it OK **(41)** .... come and see the bike after college on Thursday? I don't know **(42)** .... you live. **(43)** .... you give me your address? I'd also like to know why you **(44)** .... selling it.

From:	Ali
To:	Danny

I decided to sell the old bike **(45)** .... I got a motorbike for **(46)** .... birthday. The bike is **(47)** .... few years old but I'm sure you'll like **(48)** ....

I won't be at home on Thursday – I play football then and I don't get back until late. What about coming on Friday instead? **(49)** .... that a good day for you?

I live at 35 Portland Road, **(50)** .... to the library.

PART 8

QUESTIONS 51–55

Read the advertisement and the email.

Fill in the information on the form.

For questions 51–55, write the information on your answer sheet.

Smith's Bookshop
Book & DVD
Language Courses

Courses:	Talking Time	Speaking Plus
	Spanish	Japanese
	French	Spanish
Prices:		
Level 1:	£28.00	£30.00
Level 2:	£32.00	£35.00

From:	Tom Peters
To:	Jane Brown

My French course finished last week and I've just started learning Spanish. My teacher says the Speaking Plus course is the best. She can give me Level 1 so can you order Level 2 for me at the bookshop?

I'm at work until 6 pm. Ring me there (553905) or phone me this evening on 020 7865 4436.

Smith's Bookshop
Order Form

Customer's name:	Tom Peters
Daytime phone number:	**51**
Course name:	**52**
Language:	**53**
Level:	**54**
Price:	**55** £

PART 9

QUESTION 56

There is going to be a concert in the town where you live.
Write an email to your English friend, Elena

- **ask** her to come to the concert.

- tell her **when** the concert is.

- say **how much** the tickets are.

Write 25–35 words.
Write the email on your answer sheet.

PAPER 2   LISTENING (approximately 30 minutes including 8 minutes transfer time)

PART 1
QUESTIONS 1–5

You will hear five short conversations.

You will hear each conversation twice.

There is one question for each conversation.

For questions 1–5, put a tick (✓) under the right answer.

Example:

0   How many people were at the meeting?

3	13	30
☐	☐	☑

---

1   Where is the photograph now?

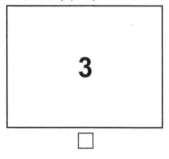

☐   ☐   ☐

2   When can Suzy come to dinner?

9th	16th	23rd

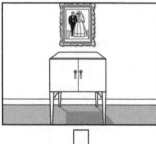  

☐   ☐   ☐

3   Where did Jane go on holiday?

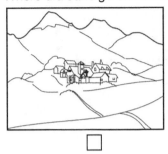  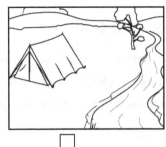

4   What has Maria hurt?

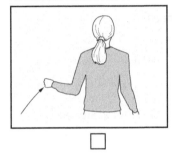  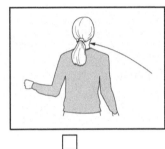

5   What time will Clare meet Jack at the station?

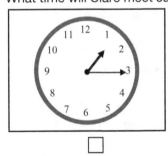 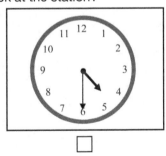 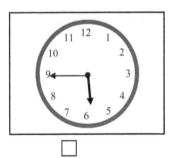

PART 2

QUESTIONS 6–10

Listen to Diana talking to a friend about the days they can do some courses.
For questions 6–10, write a letter A–H next to each day.
You will hear the conversation twice.

Example:

0 Monday

F

Days

6 Tuesday

7 Wednesday

8 Thursday

9 Friday

10 Saturday

Courses

A Business Studies

B Computer Studies

C Cooking

D Film Studies

E Geography

F Guitar

G History of Art

H The Night Sky

PART 3

QUESTIONS 11–15

Listen to a girl asking for information about a coach trip to Edinburgh.
For questions 11–15, tick (✓) A, B or C.
You will hear the conversation twice.

Example:

0	The girl wants to go to Edinburgh	A	this morning.	☐
		B	this afternoon.	☐
		C	tomorrow morning.	✓

11	The girl will pay	A	£5.	☐
		B	£7.	☐
		C	£9.	☐

12	The girl will get on the coach	A	outside the library.	☐
		B	in front of the Grand Hotel.	☐
		C	in Bridge Street.	☐

13	The coach will be at the girl's stop at	A	8.45 am.	☐
		B	8.55 am.	☐
		C	9.05 am.	☐

14 In Edinburgh, the girl will visit

    A   the castle and shops. ☐

    B   the cathedral and museums. ☐

    C   the castle and cathedral. ☐

15 The whole trip takes

    A   2 hours. ☐

    B   2¼ hours. ☐

    C   4¼ hours. ☐

PART 4

QUESTIONS 16–20

You will hear the manager of a shop leaving a message for a customer.
Listen and complete questions 16–20.
You will hear the conversation twice.

Message for Anna

From:	Bob Watson
Name of shop:	**16**
Boots:	
Size:	**17**
Colour:	**18**
Sale price:	**19** £ ....
Tomorrow shop closes at:	**20**

PART 5

QUESTIONS 21–25

You will hear a man on the radio giving information about an art class.
Listen and complete questions 21–25.
You will hear the information twice.

Art class for families

Place:	Hadley College
Date:	**21** 9th ....
Start time:	**22** .... am
Name of special guest:	**23** J.P. ....
Price of family ticket:	**24** £ ....
To book a place, call:	**25**

You now have 8 minutes to write your answers on the answer sheet.

PAPER 3   SPEAKING (8–10 minutes)

The Speaking test lasts 8 to 10 minutes. You will take the test with another candidate. There are two examiners, but only one of them will talk to you. The examiner will ask you questions and ask you to talk to the other candidate.

Part 1 (5–6 minutes)

The examiner will ask you and your partner some questions. These questions will be about your daily life, past experience and future plans. For example, you may have to speak about your school, job, hobbies or home town.

Part 2 (3–4 minutes)

You and your partner will speak to each other. You will ask and answer questions. The examiner will give you a card with some information on it. The examiner will give your partner a card with some words on it. Your partner will use the words on the card to ask you questions about the information you have. Then you will change roles.

Test 4

PAPER 1 READING AND WRITING (1 hour 10 minutes)

PART 1

QUESTIONS 1–5

Which notice (A–H) says this (1–5)?

For questions 1–5, mark the correct letter A–H on your answer sheet.

Example:

0 If you need somewhere to live soon, phone this number.

Answer:

	0	A	B	C	D	E	F	G	H
		☐	☐	☐	☐	■	☐	☐	☐

---

1 If you'd like to see this place from the air, go in the morning.

A
> CASTLE TOURS EVERY 2 HOURS
> TUES – SUN

B
> *Travellers' Hotel*
> 10 km from airport
> 44 rooms

2 Use this if you are going up to one of these apartments.

C
> Phone 552249
> to book theatre tickets
> 2pm and 8pm shows

3 Phone this company if you want to go to the airport.

D
> **Flight to catch?**
> Call Beach Taxis first on 242 242

E
> One-bedroom apartment
> to rent from next month
> Call 316606

4 It's possible to see this place at different times of the day.

F
> Park House
> This lift for apartments on floors 1–5

G
> **Helicopter flight over**
> **Dolphin Island leaves daily at 11:00**

5 There are two ways to get tickets for this.

H
> Village Concert
> pay at door or book
> tickets now on 988655

PART 2

QUESTIONS 6–10

Read the sentences about Sally's day at work.
Choose the best word (A, B or C) for each space.
For questions 6–10, mark A, B or C on your answer sheet.

Example:

0   Sally works in an office and she had a very .... day there yesterday.

  A   busy   **B**   fast   **C**   strong   *Answer:* | 0 | A ■ B ☐ C ☐ |

---

6   Sally has worked in the .... office since she left college.

  A   single   **B**   alone   **C**   same

7   Every day, Sally .... the bus to work.

  A   goes   **B**   takes   **C**   brings

8   Yesterday, Sally .... a dark blue skirt and jacket to work.

  A   had   **B**   used   **C**   wore

9   Sally .... most of her day at the office.

  A   spent   **B**   made   **C**   kept

10   Yesterday was a .... day for Sally because she had problems with her computer.

  A   difficult   **B**   tired   **C**   delayed

PART 3

QUESTIONS 11–15

Complete the five conversations.
For questions 11–15, mark A, B or C on your answer sheet.

Example:

0

Where do you come from?

A New York.

B School.

C Home.

Answer:

---

11 I'd like a cup of coffee, please.

    A Of course.

    B Yes, I do.

    C I like that.

12 Rajni's a businesswoman, isn't she?

    A Where does he work?

    B No, she can't.

    C I think so.

13 Minsk isn't in Russia.

    A Where is it then?

    B Does it have to be?

    C Isn't it somewhere?

14 Do you agree with me?

    A I haven't.

    B Certainly not.

    C No, I'm not.

15 The train has just left.

    A When did they arrive?

    B Is there another one?

    C Where are our seats?

QUESTIONS 16–20

Complete the conversation between two friends.
What does Paula say to Jenny?
For questions 16–20, mark the correct letter A–H on your answer sheet.

Example:

Jenny: It's my birthday party on Friday. Can you come?

Paula: **0** ....**C**..............   *Answer:* | **0** | A B C D E F G H |

Jenny: That's right – at eight o'clock. But I've got a lot to do before that.

Paula: **16** ....

Jenny: Well, you could come with me tomorrow to buy some food.

Paula: **17** ....

Jenny: That's a good idea. Shall we leave at about nine?

Paula: **18** ....

Jenny: Ten then. I'll come to your house and we'll leave when you're ready.

Paula: **19** ....

Jenny: Let's just buy pizza and cakes. Something quick and easy.

Paula: **20** ....

Jenny: See you tomorrow then.

A   I have to study first. How about a bit later?

B   Good idea! Everyone likes those.

C   I'd love to. Is it in the evening?

D   If you like. Do you want to go in my car?

E   Yes, I'll be there at ten.

F   What do we need to get?

G   I'm afraid I'm at work that day.

H   Would you like me to help?

PART 4

QUESTIONS 21–27

Read the article about a basketball player called Susanna Brightman.

Are sentences 21–27 'Right' (A) or 'Wrong' (B)?

If there is not enough information to answer 'Right' (A) or 'Wrong' (B), choose 'Doesn't say' (C).

For questions 21–27, mark A, B or C on your answer sheet.

Susanna Brightman

Susanna Brightman is a young Australian basketball player. She is 195 cm tall, and very fast and strong. Some people say she may become the best player in the world one day. As well as playing for her own country, she plays for a team called *Boston Hawks* in America.

Susanna was born on 15th June 1992. Her mother and father were both basketball players and when she was just 2 weeks old she was already travelling around the country with them while they played basketball. When she was still very young, Susanna told her parents she wanted to play for Australia. At the age of 16, she played for her country for the first time.

But things have not always been easy. When Susanna was 12, she toured Australia for the first time. One day, the team she was playing for lost an important match because Susanna didn't want to play. Susanna's parents were angry with her but told her that she didn't have to play basketball if she didn't want to. She needed to think hard about her future. Luckily, Susanna decided she wanted to be a basketball player after all, and since then she has worked very hard to become an even better player.

Example:

0   Susanna Brightman comes from Australia.

A   Right   **B**   Wrong   **C** Doesn't say   *Answer:* | 0 | A B C ■□□ |

---

21   Some people think Susanna is the best basketball player in the world today.

A   Right   **B**   Wrong   **C** Doesn't say

22   Susanna has won an important competition with *Boston Hawks*.

A   Right   **B**   Wrong   **C** Doesn't say

23   Susanna's parents stopped playing basketball when Susanna was born.

A   Right   **B**   Wrong   **C** Doesn't say

24   Susanna first became interested in playing basketball when she was a little child.

A   Right   **B**   Wrong   **C** Doesn't say

25   Susanna's parents asked her to stop playing basketball when she was 12.

A   Right   **B**   Wrong   **C** Doesn't say

26   Susanna gets angry when her team loses.

A   Right   **B**   Wrong   **C** Doesn't say

27   Susanna knows what she wants to do with her life.

A   Right   **B**   Wrong   **C** Doesn't say

PART 5

QUESTIONS 28–35

Read the article about kites and their history.

Choose the best word (A, B or C) for each space.

For questions 28–35, mark A, B or C on your answer sheet.

Kites

No one knows **(0)** .... made the first kite. Some
people say **(28)** .... was Archytas. He was
interested in mathematics and lived in Greece
2400 years ago.

But perhaps people in China flew kites long **(29)** .... then. Flying kites
has always been an important part of Chinese life. The ninth day of the ninth
month is a special day that is called 'The Feast of High Flight' and the sky is
full **(30)** .... kites. **(31)** .... look like fish or birds and **(32)** .... the
family joins in the fun.

Kites have a lot of different uses. Scientists used them in the 18th century
(33) .... learn about storms and other kinds of weather. At the end of the
19th century, before **(34)** .... were aeroplanes, a kite that was 11 metres
long **(35)** .... a man 30 metres up into the air!

Example:

0   **A**   who   **B**   why   **C**   when   *Answer:*   [0]   [A ■] [B □] [C □]

---

28   **A**   they   **B**   it   **C**   he

29   **A**   since   **B**   before   **C**   already

30   **A**   of   **B**   in   **C**   from

31   **A**   Both   **B**   Each   **C**   Some

32   **A**   all   **B**   other   **C**   many

33   **A**   for   **B**   by   **C**   to

34   **A**   these   **B**   there   **C**   here

35   **A**   carried   **B**   carries   **C**   carrying

PART 6

QUESTIONS 36–40

Read the descriptions of some words about reading and writing.
What is the word for each one?
The first letter is already there. There is one space for each other letter in the word.
For questions 36–40, write the words on your answer sheet.

Example:

0   You write this to your friends or family when you are
     on holiday.   **p** __ __ __ __ __ __ __

                                                        Answer: | **0** | *postcard* |

---

36   You choose from this list of food and drink
     in a restaurant.   **m** __ __ __

37   You look in this if you want to know what a word means.   **d** __ __ __ __ __ __ __ __ __

38   This person may write for a newspaper or a magazine.   **j** __ __ __ __ __ __ __ __ __

39   People who like reading enjoy going to this place.   **l** __ __ __ __ __ __

40   Some people put these on when they want to
     read something.   **g** __ __ __ __ __ __

PART 7

QUESTIONS 41–50

Complete the email.

Write ONE word for each space.

For questions 41–50, write the words on your answer sheet.

Example: | **0** | *am* |

| From: | Jan |
| To: | Monica |

Hi Monica,

I **(0)** .... writing to give you my new address – it's 24 Clifton Road. We still
live in the same city but we have just moved **(41)** .... a new house. We are
(42) .... too far from the old house so I can still see a
(43) .... of my friends. And it's easy to go to the shops **(44)** .... bus.

The new house is bigger **(45)** .... the old one and everyone likes
(46) .... There are three bedrooms – mine is **(47)** .... largest.
From the window I can just **(48)** .... the river.

(49) .... you have time, please come and visit us. Everyone will
(50) .... happy to see you.

PART 8

QUESTIONS 51–55

Read the notice and the email.

Fill in the information in Brian's notes.

For questions 51–55, write the information on your answer sheet.

Hexham College

Courses

French (Monday or Friday class)
First class: 6 December

Spanish (Wednesday or Friday class)
First class: 15 December

Cost

10 weeks – Beginners £85
                       Advanced £95
14 weeks – Beginners £105
                       Advanced £125

From:	Mick
To:	Brian

Can you book me onto a beginners language course at your college? I studied French last year so I want to try Spanish this time. I'd like to do the longer course and I have football practice on Friday, so I can't do a class then.

Brian's notes
Language course

Name of college:		Hexham College
Which language:	**51**	
Day:	**52**	
Start date:	**53**	
Number of weeks:	**54**	
Cost:	**55**	£

PART 9

QUESTION 56

Read the email from your English friend, Jools.

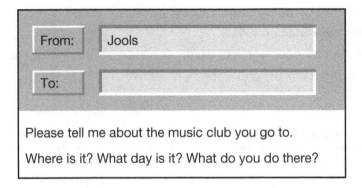

From: Jools

To:

Please tell me about the music club you go to.

Where is it? What day is it? What do you do there?

Write an email to Jools and answer the questions.

Write 25–35 words.

Write the email on your answer sheet.

PAPER 2 LISTENING (approximately 30 minutes including 8 minutes transfer time)

PART 1

QUESTIONS 1–5

You will hear five short conversations.

You will hear each conversation twice.

There is one question for each conversation.

For questions 1–5, put a tick (✓) under the right answer.

Example:

0 How many people were at the meeting?

3	13	30
☐	☐	✓

1 What is the man going to take to the repair shop?

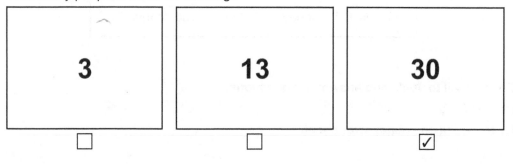

☐ ☐ ☐

2 How will Nancy and Joe get to the sports centre?

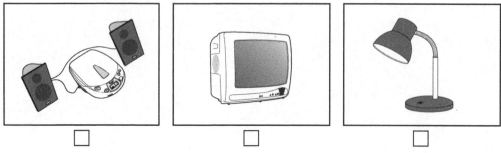

☐ ☐ ☐

3   How much is the prize for the competition?

£100	£200	£300
☐	☐	☐

4   What will the weather be like tomorrow lunchtime?

☐   ☐   ☐

5   What time will they leave home?

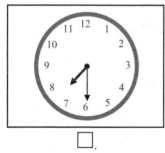  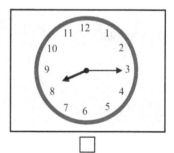

☐   ☐   ☐

PART 2

QUESTIONS 6–10

Listen to Ben talking to his wife about the clothes in his suitcase.

Which clothes will he wear each day?

For questions 6–10, write a letter A–H next to each day.

You will hear the conversation twice.

Example:

0	Sunday	D

Days

6   Monday

7   Tuesday

8   Wednesday

9   Thursday

10 Friday

Clothes

A   blue shirt

B   coat

C   jacket

D   jeans

E   light trousers

F   shorts

G   suit

H   sweater

PART 3

QUESTIONS 11–15

Listen to Duncan talking to a friend about a tennis course.
For questions 11–15, tick (✓) A, B or C.
You will hear the conversation twice.

Example:

0	How long was the tennis course?	**A** one day	☐
		B two days	☐
		C five days	✓

11	Duncan stayed in a hotel	**A** in a town.	☐
		B near the sea.	☐
		C in the mountains.	☐
12	Duncan's teacher comes from	**A** England.	☐
		B France.	☐
		C Canada.	☐
13	How much did Duncan pay for the course?	**A** £185	☐
		B £205	☐
		C £265	☐

14 Before the course, Duncan bought himself some tennis

    A shoes. ☐

    B clothes. ☐

    C balls. ☐

15 On the last evening, there was

    A a party. ☐

    B a film show. ☐

    C a tennis match. ☐

PART 4

QUESTIONS 16–20

You will hear a woman phoning for information about a boat trip.
Listen and complete questions 16–20.
You will hear the conversation twice.

Boat trip on the River Dee

Days of boat trip: Friday and Sunday

Get on boat at the: **16** _____

Time boat leaves: **17** .... pm

Boat goes to: **18** _____

On boat, you can buy: **19** drinks and ....

Cost of adult ticket: **20** £ ....

PART 5

QUESTIONS 21–25

You will hear a woman giving information on the radio about a theatre school.

Listen and complete questions 21–25.

You will hear the information twice.

Children's theatre school

Name of school: Silver Star

Cost for children over 14:   **21**   £ .... per week

Children must take their own: **22**

There is a show every: **23**

The first summer course starts   **24**   21st ....
on:

Phone number: **25**

You now have 8 minutes to write your answers on the answer sheet.

PAPER 3 SPEAKING (8–10 minutes)

The Speaking test lasts 8 to 10 minutes. You will take the test with another candidate. There are two examiners, but only one of them will talk to you. The examiner will ask you questions and ask you to talk to the other candidate.

Part 1 (5–6 minutes)

The examiner will ask you and your partner some questions. These questions will be about your daily life, past experience and future plans. For example, you may have to speak about your school, job, hobbies or home town.

Part 2 (3–4 minutes)

You and your partner will speak to each other. You will ask and answer questions. The examiner will give you a card with some information on it. The examiner will give your partner a card with some words on it. Your partner will use the words on the card to ask you questions about the information you have. Then you will change roles.

Visual materials for Paper 3

1A

Blue Sky International Airport
Opens next January

Cheap flights to the USA
8 miles from city centre
Car park for 2000 cars

2B

Picnic

- ♦ **where / picnic?**

- ♦ **date?**

- ♦ **start?** 🕐 **?**

- ♦ **what / take?**

- ♦ **music?**

3A

Fit World Sports Shop
6 Bell Street

Clothes for all sports
For adults and children
Low prices on everything
Open Monday – Saturday   9am – 5pm

4B

Job with a tour company

- ◆ **what / job?**

- ◆ **hours per day?**

- ◆ **address / company?**

- ◆ **work all year?**

- ◆ **speak other languages?**

1B

New airport

♦ **name / airport?**

♦ **where / airport?**

♦ **when / open?**

♦ **expensive flights?**

♦ **car park?**

2A

International College
Come to our summer picnic
in Victoria Park

Saturday 29th June

Dance to the music of
The Starmen

Starts 4pm
Please bring food

3B

Sports shop

♦ **open every day?**

♦ **address?**

♦ **sell tennis shoes?**

♦ **expensive?**

♦ **clothes / children?**

4A

Adventure Tours
4 Silver Street

We need a tour guide to work in
South America
September – March

*You must speak English and Spanish
Minimum 8 hours each day*

1C

CHEAP FLIGHTS
Internet bookings only: www.cheaptravel.com

London to Hong Kong
From £400 return
Every Monday
New planes with televisions and
computer games

2D

Restaurant

- name / restaurant?

- what kind / food?

- eat outside?

- good for families?

- telephone number?

3C

TOWN RUNNING RACE

Saturday 14th June

from Clifton Bridge to Market Square

for adults and children over 12 years old
Great prizes –
new sports clothes and trainers

Call 848244

4D

<u>Walk for tourists</u>

♦ **where / start?**

♦ **what / visit?**

♦ **every day?**

♦ **expensive?**

♦ **lunch?**

1D

Cheap flights

- ◆ **where / fly to?**

- ◆ **cost?**

- ◆ **fly / weekends?**

- ◆ **TV / plane?**

- ◆ **internet address?**

2C

SUMMER PALACE RESTAURANT

The best Chinese food in town!

*** Special meals for children ***

Also 10 tables in our pretty garden

To book a table – call 813729

3D

Running race

♦ **when / race?**

♦ **for everyone?**

♦ **what / win?**

♦ **where / start?**

♦ **more information? ☎ ?**

4C

City walk

Friendly guides
See the old market and castle

Starts: train station at 11 am
Finishes with lunch at Park Café

On Saturdays

All for only £15

Sample answer sheet – Reading and Writing (Sheet 1)

UNIVERSITY *of* CAMBRIDGE
ESOL Examinations

S A M P L E

Candidate Name
If not already printed, write name
in CAPITALS and complete the
Candidate No. grid (in pencil).

Candidate Signature

Examination Title

Centre

Supervisor:

If the candidate is ABSENT or has WITHDRAWN shade here ▭

Centre No.

Candidate No.

Examination
Details

0	0	0	0
1	1	1	1
2	2	2	2
3	3	3	3
4	4	4	4
5	5	5	5
6	6	6	6
7	7	7	7
8	8	8	8
9	9	9	9

KET Paper 1 Reading and Writing Candidate Answer Sheet

Instructions

Use a PENCIL (B or HB).
Rub out any answer you want to change with an eraser.

For **Parts 1, 2, 3, 4 and 5:**
Mark ONE letter for each question.
For example, if you think **C** is the right answer to the
question, mark your answer sheet like this:

0 | A B C

Part 1
1 A B C D E F G H
2 A B C D E F G H
3 A B C D E F G H
4 A B C D E F G H
5 A B C D E F G H

Part 2
6 A B C
7 A B C
8 A B C
9 A B C
10 A B C

Part 3
11 A B C
12 A B C
13 A B C
14 A B C
15 A B C

16 A B C D E F G H
17 A B C D E F G H
18 A B C D E F G H
19 A B C D E F G H
20 A B C D E F G H

Part 4
21 A B C
22 A B C
23 A B C
24 A B C
25 A B C
26 A B C
27 A B C

Part 5
28 A B C
29 A B C
30 A B C
31 A B C
32 A B C
33 A B C
34 A B C
35 A B C

Turn over for
Parts 6 - 9 →

Sample answer sheet – Reading and Writing (Sheet 2)

For **Parts 6, 7 and 8:**

Write your answers in the spaces next to the numbers (36 to 55) like this:

0	example

Part 6		Do not write here
36		1 36 0
37		1 37 0
38		1 38 0
39		1 39 0
40		1 40 0

Part 7		Do not write here
41		1 41 0
42		1 42 0
43		1 43 0
44		1 44 0
45		1 45 0
46		1 46 0
47		1 47 0
48		1 48 0
49		1 49 0
50		1 50 0

Part 8		Do not write here
51		1 51 0
52		1 52 0
53		1 53 0
54		1 54 0
55		1 55 0

Part 9 (Question 56): Write your answer below.

Do not write below (Examiner use only)
0   1   2   3   4   5

Sample answer sheet – Listening

SAMPLE

Candidate Name
If not already printed, write name
in CAPITALS and complete the
Candidate No. grid (in pencil).

Candidate Signature

Examination Title

Centre

Supervisor:
If the candidate is ABSENT or has WITHDRAWN shade here

Centre No.

Candidate No.

Examination
Details

KET Paper 2 Listening Candidate Answer Sheet

Instructions

Use a PENCIL (B or HB).

Rub out any answer you want to change with an eraser.

For **Parts 1, 2** and **3**:
Mark ONE letter for each question.
For example, if you think **C** is the right answer to the question, mark your answer sheet like this:

0 [A] [B] [C]

Part 1	Part 2	Part 3
1 A B C	6 A B C D E F G H	11 A B C
2 A B C	7 A B C D E F G H	12 A B C
3 A B C	8 A B C D E F G H	13 A B C
4 A B C	9 A B C D E F G H	14 A B C
5 A B C	10 A B C D E F G H	15 A B C

For **Parts 4** and **5**:
Write your answers in the spaces next to the
numbers (16 to 25) like this:

0 | example

Part 4		Do not write here		Part 5		Do not write here
16		1 16 0		21		1 21 0
17		1 17 0		22		1 22 0
18		1 18 0		23		1 23 0
19		1 19 0		24		1 24 0
20		1 20 0		25		1 25 0